COMPREHENSION PRACTICE

Meanings of words, nouns and verbs, making sense of sentences

Sandra Soper

A Piccolo Original
Piccolo Books

Notes for Parents

Comprehension is another word for understanding. The more a child is encouraged to think about and understand what he reads the more useful it will be.

Dictionary work has been included partly to give encouragement and practice in the use of a dictionary but also to concentrate on the meaning of single words. This is an important part of comprehension.

The passages are varied and interesting. There are everyday stories, factual descriptions, myths, limericks and ballads. These are worth reading for interest and enjoyment in their own right. The questions following the passages give the child a chance to test his understanding and perhaps encourage him to read the passage again with fresh understanding.

Midge Writes a Poem

Read the story, then answer the questions on p.5.

Midge looked out of the window at the children playing in the meadow. He'd been trying to do his homework (a poem entitled 'My Cat') for the past half hour. He had made several starts but could never get further than the second line. He glanced down at the messy page.

My cat is ~~not~~ fat
He's thin he is, ~~not~~ fat
My cat sits on the mat
He likes that, on the mat

My cat is ~~whyte~~ white
With eyes so bright
My cat
is stupid !!

"Oh, I give up." He banged his pencil down so hard on the desk that the point broke. The pencil then rolled off the edge of the desk and fell on the floor.

Midge went downstairs. Dad could tell by his face that things were not going well.

"I should leave it for now," he said, putting a hand on Midge's shoulder.

"Can I?" Midge asked incredulously.

"You can have another try after supper."

Later that evening Midge gave his cat, Marble, some milk and watched the milk disappear as he listened to the rhythmical lapping of the cat's tongue. The image stuck in his mind.

He went straight upstairs to his room, took a fresh piece of paper and wrote:

lap lap lap lap
small pink tongue
picking up the drops of milk
never spilling one
cleaning round the saucer
dainty and precise
turning now to wash himself
my cat's nice.

"Phew," he breathed out, then he read it over aloud. "Mmm, not bad, not very long, but not bad." He felt a distinct sensation of pleasure as he packed his bag. A sensation he had never before felt about poetry.

A few days later Mrs Hughes announced the names of those children who were to read their poems to the rest of the school. For the first time Midge was eager to hear the list of names, hopeful that he stood a chance. He was not disappointed. His name was first on the list. Mrs Hughes gave the children their poems so that they could be copied out in best before Friday's assembly.

Midge read his poem again. "Amazing," he said softly to himself. He stood up, smiled to himself, then went to get some paper from Mrs Hughes.

Answer these questions about the story on pages 3-4. Use sentences when you can.

How do you think Midge felt when he saw the children playing in the meadow?

What homework did Midge have to do?

Why did he bang his pencil down on the desk?

What happened to the pencil?

Was his father sympathetic or unsympathetic about his difficulties?

Try to work out what the word 'incredulously' means, then look it up in a dictionary and write down the meaning.

Which words would you use to describe Midge as he watched Marble drink the milk?
fascinated, troubled, thoughtful, soothed, amazed, interested, bored

---

How do you think Midge felt when he had finished the poem?

Near Neighbours

The missing words in each pair below are near to each other in the dictionary.
Read the clues, then use a dictionary to help you find the words.

A small Arctic rodent (**l**)	________________
A yellow citrus fruit	________________

A fruit, round at one end and narrow at the other (**p**)	________________
A milky-coloured ball found inside the shell of oysters	________________

A tool for beating, breaking, and driving nails (**h**)	________________
Cloth or netting hung by the ends for a bed or couch	________________

To falter or stutter in speech (**st**)	________________
To bring the foot forcibly to the ground	________________

A mass of tiny rounded grains of rock (**s**)	________________
A sole bound to the foot by ropes or straps	________________

Freshwater fish of the salmon family (**t**)	________________
Long breeches worn over the lower part of the body	________________

An official who rules on the playing of a game (**u**)	________________
A great many	________________

A rogue or scamp **(r)** ____________
A rare, uncommon thing ____________

To wrench or tug **(p)** ____________
A young domestic fowl ____________

Soft, wobbly pudding **(j)** ____________
Crowbar used by burglars ____________

Spoken, not written **(o)** ____________
Round, juicy citrus fruit ____________

Someone who instructs **(i)** ____________
Object which can by played to produce musical sounds ____________

Find all 24 words in the box below. Write each word out as you find it.

a	n	s	i	a	h	j	z	p	u	l	l	e	t	c	v
k	s	a	n	d	a	l	m	u	o	i	u	y	y	i	t
b	n	n	s	d	f	g	h	l	e	p	k	d	r	n	r
a	b	d	s	m	o	r	a	l	p	e	a	r	l	s	o
i	n	s	t	r	u	c	t	o	r	a	g	a	v	t	u
s	j	l	a	z	x	y	u	k	t	r	o	u	t	r	s
m	l	e	m	o	n	o	z	y	u	k	e	b	o	u	e
u	b	m	p	c	q	r	n	m	s	h	w	m	u	m	r
m	j	m	q	c	n	a	f	w	t	a	q	j	i	e	s
p	a	i	v	r	a	n	g	f	a	m	q	m	u	n	j
i	b	n	r	a	i	g	h	a	m	m	e	r	h	t	e
r	b	g	a	s	k	e	x	z	m	o	l	i	p	e	l
e	v	f	j	c	y	k	o	p	e	c	f	i	l	w	l
r	e	h	r	a	r	i	t	y	r	k	j	e	m	m	y
b	e	v	a	l	g	a	v	v	a	r	o	n	a	g	e
h	j	i	i	z	e	t	a	u	m	p	t	e	e	n	m

1 ____________
2 ____________
3 ____________
4 ____________
5 ____________
6 ____________
7 ____________
8 ____________
9 ____________
10 ____________
11 ____________
12 ____________
13 ____________
14 ____________
15 ____________
16 ____________
17 ____________
18 ____________
19 ____________
20 ____________
21 ____________
22 ____________
23 ____________
24 ____________

Tortoise Tale

This is a myth from Africa where people invented stories (as they did in most parts of the world) to explain some of the huge variety of features and shapes of the animals around them.

Why the shell of the tortoise is cracked and the waist of the wasp is tiny.

Long, long ago, when all the creatures could talk like you and me, the birds of the forest decided to have a party in the tree tops. Tortoise overheard two parrots talking about the wonderful food being gathered together. Naturally he wanted to go to the party too. But there was one problem. Tortoise couldn't fly.

The birds were discussing how to solve the problem, when the mockingbird came up with an idea. Each bird would take one of its feathers and stick it on Tortoise's shell. When this was done, he looked glorious and, with the help of the birds, he reached the tree tops without difficulty.

During the party, the birds played the game 'Change-my-name', in which each creature was allowed to chose a new name. Tortoise, who had played the game before, chose the name 'You-all'. After the party there were, as always, lots of jobs to be done to clear up. Whenever You-all was called to do a job, everyone started to help. Eventually the birds noticed how they had been tricked and immediately took their feathers back. In a few minutes Tortoise hadn't a single feather on his shell. How was he to get down to the ground below?

Wasp, who had seen and heard everything, thought she would teach Tortoise a further lesson. She offered to build him a soft landing if he would share some of his party food with her. Tortoise agreed. Wasp flew down and built a mound of stones which she covered with moss.

When Tortoise landed on the mound, of course his shell broke into pieces. Wasp didn't intend to leave him like that. She wanted only to improve his manners. Besides, she wanted her share of the party food. Using the paper paste with which she made her nest, she quickly had Tortoise back together again. He was still furious and, walking over to Wasp, he picked her up, pulled her apart, then quickly stuck her together again.

"There, now we are equal and I owe you nothing. I shall have all the food to myself." He turned to pick up the food, only to find it had gone. A moment before, some monkeys had come by. They could hardly believe their good fortune when they saw the pile of food and vanished with it up to the tree tops, where they had a delicious and unexpected feast.

Answer these questions.

Which continent does this story come from? Which hemisphere is it in?

____

Which two things does the story try to explain?

____

How did the birds help Tortoise to get to the treetops?

____

How did the birds react when they saw they'd been tricked?

____

Why did Wasp cover the stones to trick Tortoise?

____

Do you think Wasp and Tortoise got what they deserved?

____

Limericks

A limerick is a five line verse which has the rhyming pattern, a a b b a. Read these limericks aloud.

There was a young lady of Riga
Who went for a ride on a tiger
They returned from the ride
With the lady inside
And the smile on the face of the tiger

Edward Lear

There was an old miser at Reading
Had a house and a yard with a shed in
'Twas meant for a cow
But so small that I vow
The poor creature could scarce get her head in

Anon

There was a young girl in the choir
Whose voice arose higher and higher
Till one Sunday night
It rose quite out of sight
And they found it next day on the spire

Anon

There was a young princess from Gloucester
Whose parents thought they had lost her
At last safe and sound
In the fridge she was found
But the problem was how to defrost her

Danny Seggar, aged 10

Write your answers to these questions, using a sentence each time.

Why do you think the tiger was smiling?

What was the miser's shed supposed to be?

On which night did the girl's voice disappear?

Where was the lost princess found?

In which two limericks is something lost, then found?

In which limerick does something vanish completely?

Explain, in your own words, the meaning of a miser.

Write your own limerick here.

Lottie's Rubber

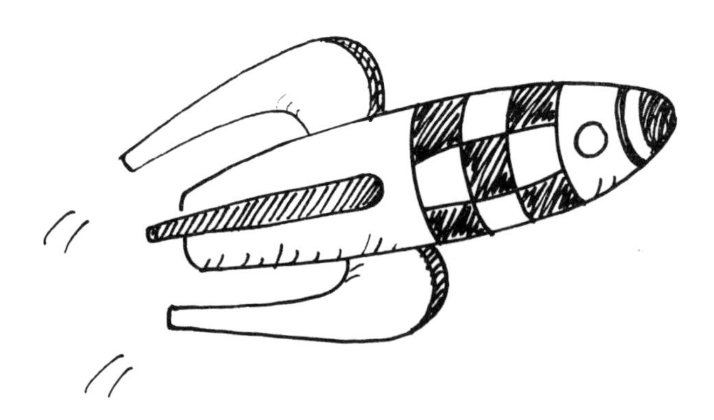

Lottie was complaining loudly that her space missile rubber had vanished.
"I'm sure I put it in here," she said, rummaging for the third time in the kitchen drawer. "I remember tucking it behing the red box."
"If you put it there, it should still be there," said Mum. "And don't frown at me like that. I've told you before, *your* things are *your* responsibility."
"I bet Midge has taken it," said Lottie.
"Now, don't jump to any conclusions."
"But mum, I saw him swapping with Tony this morning and I know that Tony is collecting rubbers. I *promised* Petra that I would bring it this afternoon. We were going to time ourselves taking it apart and putting it together again. Oh I *wish* people would leave my things alone!" She opened the drawer for one last look, banged it shut, then stomped off upstairs. . .
A few minutes later Midge appeared in the kitchen."Can I have an apple, Mum? I'm starving." He took an apple from the bowl without waiting for a reply.
"Have you seen Lottie's missing rubber?" asked Mum. "She seems to think it has vanished from that drawer."
"Crumbs, that's her favourite rubber," said Midge.
"Yes, and she thinks you might have taken it."
"*Me*?" asked Midge in surprise.
"You have taken her things before without permission," Mum reminded him.
"Honestly Mum, I didn't take that rubber."
Mrs O'Neil looked at her son. She could tell by his expression that he was telling the truth.

Answer these questions, using sentences when you can.

Why was Lottie looking in the kitchen drawer?

Why was she so angry?

What do you think Mrs O'Neil meant by saying, '*Your* things are *your* responsibility?'

What conclusion did Lottie jump to when she couldn't find what she was looking for?

Did she have any evidence to back up this conclusion?

What had she and Petra planned to do that afternoon?

How would you describe Lottie's feelings as she went upstairs?

Was Mrs O'Neil convinced or not that Midge was telling the truth?

Invent an ending to the story in which the rubber is found.

Sports and Hobbies

t	e	n	n	i	s	a	i	l	i	n	g	s	h	c	h	e	s	s	l
g	a	v	d	o	q	u	i	l	t	i	n	g	t	z	m	w	e	k	s
j	h	r	f	l	u	c	j	y	t	p	q	w	h	g	u	o	w	i	w
b	v	c	r	e	a	d	i	n	g	a	l	k	e	c	s	k	i	i	r
y	u	l	s	w	s	w	i	m	m	i	n	g	a	s	i	x	n	n	i
e	v	v	h	j	h	a	d	j	k	n	m	r	i	r	c	t	g	g	t
f	o	o	t	b	a	l	l	b	v	t	a	d	j	k	r	d	w	m	i
s	t	z	c	o	o	k	i	n	g	i	b	a	d	m	i	n	t	o	n
k	c	y	u	w	l	i	m	o	p	n	g	a	r	d	e	n	i	n	g
a	z	t	l	o	q	n	x	r	u	g	g	y	p	e	w	a	c	v	n
t	g	d	w	k	w	g	o	l	f	j	k	n	i	t	t	i	n	g	u
e	b	o	a	r	d	i	n	g	j	s	a	c	l	i	m	b	i	n	g

Find these sports or hobbies in the box above.

tennis
chess
squash
quilting
swimming
football
walking
cooking
gardening
badminton

reading
knitting
skiing
sewing
skate-boarding
painting
music

climbing
writing
sailing

Read each question, then write an answer in the box.

Which sport has its major championship at Wimbledon each summer?

Which hobby needs only a good book and a comfy chair?

Which sport can also be a fruit drink?

In which sport is a shuttlecock hit over a net?

For which sport is snow essential?

In which hobby can you use needle, cloth and thread to make something to wear?

In which sport does the wind play a major part?

Millions of people are interested in sports and hobbies. Only the gifted and dedicated few can make a life out of an interest. For which are the following people famous?

Fatima Whitbread

Steffi Graff

Edmund Hilary

Picasso

Beatrix Potter

Madonna

Wolfgang Mozart

Roald Dahl

Near Neighbours

The missing words in each pair below are near to each other in the dictionary. Read the clues, then use the dictionary to help you find the words.

Soft, squishy and damp earthy matter **(m)**	____________
Mess or disorder	____________

Minced meat forced into cylindrical skin **(s)**	____________
To fry food quickly in hot fat	____________

Woody plant smaller than a tree **(sh)**	____________
To raise shoulders to show indifference	____________

Tall, stately wading bird **(s)**	____________
Violent disturbance in the weather	____________

Naughty sprite said to cause faults in machinery **(g)**	____________
Small explosive shell thrown by hand	____________

Thin, crumbly biscuit made of oatmeal **(o)**	____________
A solemn pledge or promise	____________

To stamp roughly on **(t)**	____________
Tough canvas sheet suspended by springs	____________

A simple country lad **(y)**
The central part of an egg

Art of working in wood **(c)** ____________________

Heavy fabric for covering floors ____________________

The highest point **(z)** ____________________

A soft gentle breeze ____________________

Tool for loosening soil, scraping up weeds **(h)** ____________________

Domestic pig, especially male, reared for slaughter ____________________

To shout or scream **(y)** ____________________

Sunny colour ____________________

Find all 24 words in the box below. Write each word out as you find it.

a	g	h	m	k	f	g	k	l	p	u	u	z	a	s	d	d	q	m	n	i	o	p
x	c	a	r	p	e	n	t	r	y	a	e	w	v	s	o	s	g	z	l	f	g	f
e	r	t	y	u	i	o	p	z	x	c	v	b	h	j	x	k	r	a	a	o	w	q
d	f	h	m	q	s	v	b	n	w	a	k	m	u	d	d	l	e	s	h	t	f	h
r	c	q	n	m	h	j	k	y	r	c	m	u	k	e	x	o	n	e	a	r	i	o
k	l	e	x	z	r	p	o	e	y	j	s	d	j	d	f	o	a	t	c	a	k	e
t	x	m	s	a	u	s	a	g	e	d	g	n	a	u	c	o	d	z	a	m	t	k
s	d	q	a	j	b	i	t	f	p	m	c	a	z	n	s	x	e	i	a	p	x	k
s	h	r	u	g	j	l	h	a	n	j	w	q	e	d	n	v	i	l	r	o	e	p
f	x	u	t	m	n	e	m	i	w	q	j	c	p	z	a	k	j	y	e	l	z	p
u	y	v	é	g	w	v	o	r	e	f	x	d	h	i	o	e	x	g	b	i	a	p
x	s	e	j	m	c	o	q	l	g	h	w	x	y	n	s	t	o	r	k	n	m	z
g	k	e	l	s	o	p	p	x	l	y	b	d	r	e	t	x	a	e	z	e	u	r
d	h	u	c	l	p	m	y	o	k	e	l	n	w	y	o	l	k	m	g	a	v	d
f	d	o	p	c	a	k	b	x	p	l	k	e	a	l	r	r	p	l	d	e	f	t
j	x	r	l	r	b	k	l	m	f	l	v	s	w	i	m	l	w	i	q	t	a	o
l	r	b	t	k	n	u	o	p	m	o	f	s	d	e	g	b	f	n	e	o	p	x
g	s	j	c	l	k	m	b	z	i	w	h	s	z	a	n	j	o	p	f	q	b	y
h	x	r	x	n	t	i	u	v	b	l	o	k	r	z	j	w	r	e	o	q	c	t
r	b	n	i	z	e	n	i	t	h	d	k	w	a	h	o	a	f	c	i	r	o	l
n	b	i	e	z	o	p	m	k	d	k	a	b	l	e	c	e	a	m	n	r	w	g

1 ____________
2 ____________
3 ____________
4 ____________
5 ____________
6 ____________
7 ____________
8 ____________
9 ____________
10 ____________
11 ____________
12 ____________
13 ____________
14 ____________
15 ____________
16 ____________
17 ____________
18 ____________
19 ____________
20 ____________
21 ____________
22 ____________
23 ____________
24 ____________

Alabama

This poem was written by a North American Indian. Read it aloud and colour the illustration.

My brethren,
among the legends of my people
it is told how a chief,
leading the remnant of his people,
crossed a great river,
and striking his tipi-stake upon the ground,
exclaimed, "A-la-ba-ma!"
This in our language means
"Here we may rest!"
But he saw not the future.
The white man came:
he and his people could not rest there;
they were driven out,
and in a dark swamp
they were thrust down in to the slime
and killed.
The word he so sadly spoke
has given a name to one of the white man's states.
There is no spot under those stars
that now smile upon us,
where the Indian can plant his foot
and sigh "A-la-ba-ma."

Khe-tha-a-hi (Eagle Wing)

Answer these questions, using sentences when you can.

What does Khe-tha-a-hi mean in English?

In the poem we are told the chief led the remnant (or remains) of his people. What do you suppose happened to the rest?

Describe what a tipi-stake is and how it is used.

What did the chief mean when he exclaimed "A-la-ba-ma?"

Explain why these words proved not to be true.

Do you think the white people had a right to act as they did?

Alabama is one of the United States of America. Write the names of three other states.

Write in your own words what the author is saying in the last four lines of the poem.

The Human Body

The skeleton is the solid frame on which the human body is built. It is a protection for the vital organs of the body and is also a firm base to which organs and muscles can be attached. The bones of the body are connected by a flexible pearly white substance called cartilage, which can be torn or damaged by a sudden awkward movement of a joint.

The most important bone in the body is the spinal column. It is made up of separate pieces called vertebrae. In between each vertebrae is a soft disc which helps movement and also acts as a shock absorber.

The body moves when muscles act upon the skeleton. There are three types of muscle: cardiac, smooth and striped. Cardiac muscle, as its name implies, is found only in the heart. Smooth muscles are found in the walls of arteries and intestines. The most common muscle in the body is the striped. It consists of a fibre, (which is made up of minute threads) surrounded by a sheath. A complete muscle is made up of bundles of fibres covered by a membrane.

The muscles are attached to bones by cords of tough tissue called tendons. Each muscle fibre has a nerve ending connected to it. The muscle fibre contracts when it is stimulated by its individual nerve. It then relaxes until it is stimulated again. Muscles which bend a joint are called flexors; those which straighten it out are known as extensors.

Answer the questions, using sentences when you can.

Describe the two main functions of the skeleton.

How are the bones of the body connected to each other?

What is the most important bone in the body?

Why are there soft discs between the vertebrae?

Name the three types of muscle in the body.

Where is the cardiac muscle found?

What are tendons?

What makes a muscle contract?

Explain the difference between flexors and extensors.

Eggie Bread

"Have you ever had French toast?" Petra asked. She and Lottie had just woken up. They often slept with each other during the holidays.

"Is it like eggie bread?"

"Mmm I think so," Petra put on her TV announcer's voice. "First take a bowl and into this break one or two eggs for each person. Add some milk and a little salt and pepper. Whisk the mixture with a fork for a few minutes. Take one to two slices of bread for each person and dip in the mixture till the bread is saturated. Carefully lift out and put on a plate. Now heat some oil in a frying pan. When the fat is hot, gently place the bread in the pan. Fry on both sides till golden brown, remove from the pan and store in a warm overn until ready to serve."

By the end of this, Lottie's mouth was watering. "Shall we go and make some for the others as a surprise?"

"Great idea!" Petra said. She jumped out of bed.

They crept down to the kitchen and started. The fat was heating in the frying pan when the phone went. It was Petra's brother – she'd taken his sleeping bag and he was furious. He needed it to go off camping. She must bring it back there and then. Just as Petra was squeezing out of the front door, Lottie's mum appeared. "What's going on?" she whispered, "and what's that burning smell?"

Lottie ran to the kitchen. It was thick with black smoke. Mum came in, grabbed the pan and doused it in cold water. Hissing steam everywhere.

"Sorry, Mum. We wanted to surprise you."

Mrs O'Neil was banging saucepans and plates around. "You make sure you know what you're doing in future. How many eggs did you use? Look at this soggy mess! There's enough here to feed the whole street."

Lottie loved her mum, but she wished she'd try to see her side of things sometimes.

Answer these questions, using sentences when you can.

What is another name for eggie bread?

Approximately what time do you think the girls woke up?

How do we know the story takes place in the school holdiays?

What is the minimum number of eggs required to make eggie bread for six people?

Why do you think the bread has to be placed gently in the pan?

Why did the girls creep to the kitchen?

When the telephone rang, who was on the line?

Write out a conversation between Lottie and Petra later that day. Start like this:

L: That was a fine time to go off I must say.

P:

Volcanoes

A volcanic region is one where the earth's crust is relatively thin. Rocks under pressure from a heavy weight above have a much higher melting point than rocks which do not have this pressure. So even after the earth's crust had set solid there were, and still are, pockets of molten rock beneath the thin patches of crust. This molten rock gets squeezed into all the cracks and crannies which surround the pocket. Sometimes a crack reaches right up to the surface and a fountain of molten rock is squirted up into the air. This is a volcano.

The molten rock that comes out of a volcano is called lava. When it cools it may form lumps of glassy rock, but more often it is a sort of rock froth full of bubbles of gas, which cools to form pumice. Wherever the lava falls or flows it destroys everything in its path. Sometimes whole towns have been wiped out.

Volcanoes are usually in the form of a conical mountain with a hole running down its centre. The opening to the hole is widened by the constant explosions and the overflow of lava which creates a bowl-shaped hollow or crater at the top of the volcano.

A volcano is like a kind of safety valve. Once the lava has erupted, the pressure is reduced below and the volcano becomes dormant, sometimes for many years, before the pressure builds up again. Some volcanoes are always smoking and erupt every few weeks or months, but these eruptions are fairly minor. The unexpected eruption from pressure built up over several years is the one most likely to cause the greatest amount of death and destruction.

A volcano which is not expected to be active again is described as extinct.

Write your answers using sentences when you can.

Will a rock with a high melting point melt quicker or slower than a rock with a low melting point?

Do rocks below the thin part of the earth's crust bear more or less pressure than those below the thick part?

Describe a volcanic eruption in your own words.

What is lava?

Explain how a volcano acts as a kind of safety valve.

What is the difference between an active and a dormant volcano?

Look up 'pumice' in a dictionary and write a definition here.

Near Neighbours

The missing words in each pair are near to each other in the dictionary. Read the clues, then use a dictionary to help you find the words.

Member of a North American Indian people (**A**)	________________
Separate or away from each other	________________

Appreciation shown by clapping hands (**a**)	________________
Shiny-skinned fruit with crisp white flesh	________________

Middle of the day (**n**)	________________
A corner or narrow recess	________________

Mischievous or disobedient (**n**)	________________
A feeling of sickness	________________

An adult female human being (**w**)	________________
The plural of wolf	________________

A small model of a human being used as a toy (**d**)	________________
Standard unit of money in USA divided into 100 cents	________________

Percussion instrument to beat and shake (**t**)	________________
Animals not wild or dangerous or afraid of humans	________________

Knee-length pleated skirt usually in plaid or tartan (**k**) ____________

Sashed ankle-length garment worn in Japan ____________

(Of weather) mild, pleasant (**b**) ____________

Foolish talk, nonsense ____________

Pointless, trifling (**f**) ____________

The time yet to come ____________

Sound made by a duck (**q**) ____________

Short for 'quadrangle' ____________

Find all 22 words in the box below. Write each word out as you find it.

1 ____________ 2 ____________ 3 ____________

4 ____________ 5 ____________ 6 ____________

c	d	g	j	k	d	g	s	m	i	A	l	t	s	b	c	x	o	p	y	a	z
v	w	o	l	v	e	s	k	r	p	p	h	j	q	m	k	k	t	t	m	s	z
k	p	o	z	k	j	r	s	c	b	a	p	a	r	t	c	n	h	z	a	b	i
n	g	k	m	a	q	c	u	f	s	c	j	q	u	a	d	g	d	k	f	h	w
x	s	t	b	a	l	m	y	k	s	h	k	c	u	m	u	j	d	a	u	o	h
c	g	s	k	u	n	s	y	k	l	e	z	q	k	a	y	x	p	w	t	b	i
j	k	v	z	o	p	e	d	o	t	w	z	m	n	a	u	s	e	a	u	k	l
p	i	a	p	p	l	a	u	s	e	f	g	n	c	d	x	v	m	n	r	s	u
t	m	l	p	a	g	j	r	d	l	u	e	d	i	o	p	t	a	m	e	g	u
p	o	c	v	p	x	s	f	j	k	n	h	z	q	t	y	b	c	u	r	e	f
f	n	h	b	g	l	a	s	f	i	q	g	a	v	v	a	k	j	l	r	t	u
u	o	e	t	a	c	e	z	r	j	k	o	z	d	o	l	l	f	u	i	p	t
d	h	j	w	b	l	t	u	l	s	v	p	d	o	l	l	a	r	d	s	y	i
w	g	x	u	i	j	o	d	q	z	j	k	n	o	o	n	h	t	y	s	z	l
h	i	t	e	g	b	j	n	c	s	t	y	n	o	x	t	r	s	w	a	m	e
f	g	j	i	m	z	a	e	e	g	u	i	s	q	o	n	k	l	f	u	i	o
e	a	t	a	x	g	u	o	p	y	x	q	i	o	p	k	i	l	t	e	r	c
y	h	t	t	r	v	b	n	u	i	m	q	a	p	o	k	h	g	k	l	r	s

7 ____________

8 ____________

9 ____________

10 ____________

11 ____________

12 ____________

13 ____________

14 ____________

15 ____________

16 ____________

17 ____________

18 ____________

19 ____________

20 ____________

21 ____________

22 ____________

The Female Highwayman

Read the poem aloud, then colour the illustration.

Priscilla on one summer's day
Dressed herself up in men's array;
With a brace of pistols by her side
To meet her true love she did ride.

And when she saw her true love there
She boldly bade him for to stand.
"Stand and deliver, kind sir," she said,
"For if you don't I'll shoot you dead."

And when she'd robbed him of all his store,
Said she, "Kind sir, there's one thing more;
The diamond ring I've seen you wear,
Deliver that and your life I'll spare."

"That ring," said he, "my true love gave;
My life I'll lose but that I'll save."
Then, being tender-hearted like a dove,
She rode away from the man she love.

Anon they walked upon the green,
And he spied his watch pinned to her clothes,
Which made her blush, which made her blush
Like a full, blooming rose.

"'Twas me who robbed you on the plain,
So here's your watch and your gold again.
I did it only for to see
If you would really faithful be.
And now I'm sure that this is true,
I also gave my heart to you."

Write your answers, using sentences when you can.

Who is Priscilla?

How many pistols are in a brace?

What is 'men's array'?

Why did Priscilla dress up?

What does 'stand and deliver' mean?

Why did the man refuse to give up his diamond ring?

Explain how the identity of the Female Highwayman was discovered.

What was her explanation of her actions?

Riddles

Read each riddle, then write the answers in the boxes. Illustrate the riddles. (You will find the answers on the back cover.)

I fly -
like a bird
and buzz
like a bee
got a tail like a fish
got a hop like a flea.

Looking through the window
seeing a miracle,
water become glass.

I am the terror of mankind,
my breath is flame and by its power
I urge my messenger to find
a way into the strongest tower.

A skin have I,
more eyes than one,
I can be tasty when I am done.

Use it all over
from head to toes,
the more you use,
the less it grows.

Little Lucy Etticoat
in a white petticoat
and a yellow nose,
the longer she stands,
the shorter she grows.

Four fingers and a thumb,
yet flesh and blood
have I none.

This is an old English ballad. Read it through, then answer the questions.

Get Up and Bar the Door

It fell about the Martinmas time.
And a gay time it was then,
When our goodwife got puddings to make,
And she boiled them in the pan.

The wind so cold blew south and north,
And blew into the floor;
Quoth our goodman to our goodwife,
'Get up and bar the door.'

'My hand is on my household work,
Goodman, as ye may see;
And it will not be barred for a hundred years
If it's to be barred by me!

They made a pact between them both,
They made it firm and sure,
That whoso'er should speak the first,
Should rise and bar the door.

Then by there came two gentlemen,
At twelve o'clock at night,
And they could see neither house nor hall,
nor coal nor candlelight.

'Now whether this is a rich man's house.
Or whether it is a poor?'
But never a word would one of them speak
For barring of the door.

The guests they ate the white puddings,
And then they ate the black;
Tho' much the goodwife thought to herself,
Yet never a word she spake.

Then said one stranger to the other,
'Here, man, take my knife;
You take off the old man's beard,
And I'll kiss his wife.'

'There's no hot water to scrape it off,
And what shall we do then?'
'Then why not use the pudding broth,
That boils inside the pan?'

O up then started our goodman,
An angry man was he;
'Will you kiss my wife before my eyes
And with pudding broth scald me!'

Then up and started our goodwife,
Gave three skips on the floor:
'Goodman you have spoken the first word!
Get up and bar the door!'

Why did the wife object to her husband asking her to bar the door?

What was the pact they made between them?

When the guests arrived, what did they say?

What was to be used for hot water to shave the old man's beard?

Write out an explanation of the last two verses in your own words.
